This
book belongs to

...a wife after
God's own heart.

A Wife After God's Own Heart

Elizabeth George

HARVEST HOUSE PUBLISHERS

EUGENE, OREGON

Cover by Garborg Design Works, Minneapolis, Minnesota

Cover photo © Denis Boissavy/Getty Images

Acknowledgment

As always, thank you to my dear husband, Jim George, M.Div., Th.M., for your able assistance, guidance, suggestions, and loving encouragement on this project.

A WIFE AFTER GOD'S OWN HEART GROWTH AND STUDY GUIDE
Copyright © 2004 by Elizabeth George
Published by Harvest House Publishers
Eugene, Oregon 97402
www.harvesthousepublishers.com

ISBN 0-7369-1168-5

Printed in the United States of America

04 05 06 07 08 09 10 11 /BP-KB/ 10 9 8 7 6 5 4 3 2 1

Contents

A Word of Welcome

Please let me welcome you to this helpful, fun, and most practical growth and study guide for women like you who are married and desire to be even better wives after God's own heart. To you I say, *Bravo!* Your choice to take your hopes and dreams to a higher level—to put in the time to seriously apply the guidelines discussed in this study and incorporate the many "little things" that can improve your marriage on a daily basis—will most definitely pay off. How?

- 🎗 *You* will have the satisfaction of knowing you are doing things God's way. Plus...

- 🎗 *Your husband* will be blessed as you devote yourself to the 12 areas that really matter in a marriage. And just possibly...and probably...

- 🎗 *Your marriage* will dramatically change and improve.

A Word of Instruction

The exercises in this study guide are easy to do. And the best thing is that they center around the issues and concerns of your daily life as a wife. You'll need your copy of the book *A Wife After God's Own Heart,* your Bible, a pen, a dictionary, and a heart ready to tackle the challenge of improving as a wife. In each lesson you'll be asked to:

    ❦   Read the corresponding chapter from *A Wife After God's Own Heart.*

    ❦   Answer the questions designed to help you better understand and live out God's guidelines for you as a wife.

    ❦   Write out your own heart commitments along the way.

    ❦   Begin applying God's Word immediately by selecting one "little thing" you can do to improve your marriage.

A Word for Your Group

Of course, you can grow as a wife as you work your way, alone, through the biblical principles and the "little things that make a big difference" presented in this book and apply them to your life. But I urge you to share the rich and life-changing journey with other women—with your friends, your neighbors, your Sunday school class, and women's Bible study. A group, no matter how small or large, offers personal care and adds interest. There is sharing. There are sisters-in-Christ to pray for you. There is the mutual exchange of experiences. There is account-ability. And, yes, there is peer pressure—which always helps us get our lessons done so that glorious growth occurs! And there is sweet, sweet encouragement as you share God's Word with one another and as, together, you stimulate one another to greater love and good works.

To aid the woman who is guided by God to lead a group, I've included a section in the back of this growth and study guide entitled "Leading a Bible Study Discussion Group." You may also find this information and more on my website: www.elizabethgeorge.com.

A Word of Encouragement

What is it worth, dear one, to have a heart and a home that honor God and are pleasing in His eyes? Is it worth spending a few minutes a day or a few hours in a week internalizing the principles found in *A Wife After God's Own Heart* and in this growth and study guide? What I'm offering you is the opportunity to take what you're learning to a deeper level and to work it out in your life and marriage—to live out what you know you want to do and be...a wife after God's own heart!

If you will use the insights, tools, and how-to's gained from the book *A Wife After God's Own Heart* and from this study guide, by God's grace and with His help, your husband—and others!—will notice a difference and begin to describe *you* as a woman after God's own heart. Your ways will be more gracious, constructive, wise, and most of all, exhibit the inner person of the heart who is very precious in the sight of God (1 Peter 3:4).

1

Growing in the Lord

In your copy of *A Wife After God's Own Heart*, read the opening chapter entitled "Growing in the Lord." What meant the most to you as a married woman?

I would like for God to be the #1 difference in my life

What offered you the greatest challenge as a wife?

To follow hard after Him and close behind him. I get so wrapped up in the moment.

What information was new or served as a fresh reminder for you as you seek to follow after God's own heart in your marriage?

the three steps

Introductory Section

*"A relationship with God through Jesus Christ
is the key to all of life,
including your marriage!"*

What is your story about how you began growing in the Lord?

Andrew my son first led me to the Lord. I felt so awesome when I would go to church, I love the feeling of the Lord.

Can you list a few changes a strengthened relationship with God has made in your marriage so far?

this is the first time, when Adam went to church with me I felt as solid as rock. I know I was glowin

First Things First

> *"Every Christian wife is to put first things first—*
> *to seek the Lord first and foremost—*
> *because God expects every Christian to grow."*

Look at these verses in your Bible, and note what each says about spiritual growth.

Matthew 6:33—

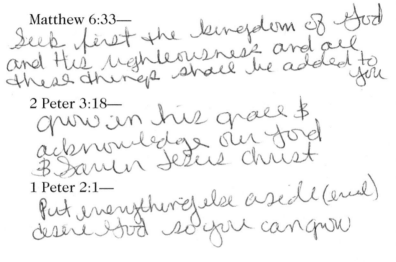

Seek first the kingdom of God and His righteousness and all these things shall be added to you

2 Peter 3:18—

grow in his grace & acknowledge our Lord & Savior Jesus Christ

1 Peter 2:1—

Put everything else aside (end) desire God so you can grow

Hebrews 5:12-13—

Maturity comes from practice

Take a minute to write a sentence or two describing your hunger for the pure milk and solid food of the Word of God. Do any changes need to take place? What are they?

I want to live for the Lord in every way, actions, thoughts, words heart

How's Your Heart?

"If there is a holy desire to grow in the Lord,
to be a woman after His heart,
then let your heart be soft and responsive to God."

In your own words, describe a woman and a wife after God's own heart according to...

Psalm 63:8—

God supports us daily he is with us always

Acts 13:22—

God saw a deep desire to do his will in David throughout his entire life he was selfwilled

Romans 12:2—

form a mold, be transformed mind & heart dedicated to gods truth

Psalm 139 offers help for the heart that desires to follow after God. What do verses 23-24 say you can do to constantly improve your heart?

Ask God to examine your thoughts & purge us of our sin so we can have everlasting life

Deciding to Grow

*"The most important thing you must decide
to do each and every day of your life
is to put the Lord first."*

Do you agree or disagree that you are in the driver's seat concerning most of the structure of your every day, including your growth in the Lord? Why or why not?

I do now and would like to make a life change

What decisions have you, "the driver," been making about your spiritual growth?

Taking this class and hopefully a wed morning class + church

What falls under the "Needs Improvement" column in your spiritual life?

the way I speak, think studying the Bible

How do you think improving your growth in the Lord will improve your marriage?

I believe through God all things are possible

Tending Your Growth

> *"Just as any skill or talent*
> *requires careful attention,*
> *so does your precious and priceless*
> *spiritual growth."*

Spiritual growth results from discipline—To run the Christian race and to be God's kind of wife requires that you "train diligently" and put forth daily "hard work, self-denial, and grueling preparation." How can you turn up the heat on your efforts for such personal discipline...

...today?

self denial is huge.

...this week?

grueling preparation

Spiritual growth results from self-denial—What are some of your "special duties" as a wife?

to prepare myself to take care & love my husband

And what must you give up in order to do what God wants of you as a wife?

selfishness

Reaping God's Blessings

"As you grow in the Lord,
you'll be a better wife."

Other than your relationship with God, as a married woman the most powerful, satisfying blessing you can enjoy is that of a strong, healthy, and improving relationship with your day-in day-out companion, your husband. As you've focused on growing in the Lord, can you give one instance how you've seen...

...your behavior change?

Thying to be more lovsing and less judgemental

...your relationship with your husband change?

he is less frustrated when d am less judemental & lovvng

Heart Response

"We only need to know what God says
is the basic recipe for being
a woman and a wife after His own heart
...and to faithfully follow His recipe."

Think now about your marriage and your life. Then write
out in 100 words or less your aspirations for your spiritual
growth, and seal it with a time of prayer.

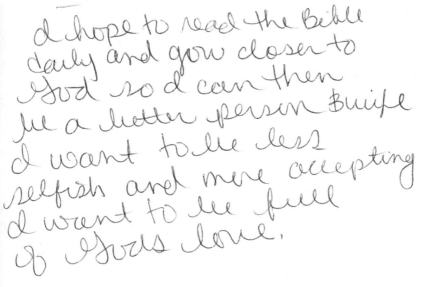

I hope to read the Bible
daily and grow closer to
God so I can then
be a better person & wife
I want to be less
selfish and more accepting
I want to be full
of God's love.

Little Things That Make a Big Difference

Look again at the section in this chapter entitled "Little Things That Make a Big Difference." Because growing in the Lord really matters in your marriage, what one "little thing" can you do this week to promote your growth in the Lord? Write it here...and don't forget to note the fantastic results!

I will...

read the bible

Thank You, God, for the following changes, blessings, and results...

for helping to find this class & MOPS I know wonderful changes and blessings will be the result.

2

Working as a Team

 In your copy of *A Wife After God's Own Heart,* read the chapter entitled "Working as a Team." What meant the most to you as a married woman?

What offered you the greatest challenge as a wife?

What information was new or served as a fresh reminder for you as you seek to follow after God's own heart in your marriage?

God's Winning Combination

> *"When God surveyed His remarkable handiwork*
> *on Day Six of Creation,*
> *one more thing was needed—*
> *a helper and a companion."*

As you look in your Bible at these verses, write down their messages about a winning combination in marriage.

A husband is to lead in his marriage and family.

       Genesis 3:16—

       Ephesians 5:22-23—

       Colossians 3:18—

A husband is to work and to provide for his wife.

       Genesis 3:17-19—

A husband is to love his wife.

       Ephesians 5:25—

       Ephesians 5:28—

       Colossians 3:19—

       1 Peter 3:7—

A wife is to help her husband.

> Genesis 2:18—

A wife is to submit to her husband.

> Ephesians 5:22—

> Colossians 3:18—

> 1 Peter 3:1—

A wife is to respect her husband.

> Ephesians 5:33—

A wife is to love her husband.

> Titus 2:3-4—

Following God's Plan

*"God's recipe for a happy marriage
contains four basic ingredients—
a helping hand, a submissive spirit,
a respectful manner, and a loving heart."*

What kind of wife are you? Are you a "husband-watcher," quick to criticize and point out your husband's faults and shortcomings? Are you assuming a "when...then" attitude, waiting for your partner to do his part? Every wife slips up once in a while, but if this is the pattern for your relationship with your husband, how does Titus 2:4-5 motivate you to quickly begin following God's plan?

Or are you a wife after God's own heart who is seeking first and foremost to follow His plan for your part of your marriage? Are you desiring to know God's guidelines for you as a wife...and to implement them on a daily basis? Look now at Romans 12:2. How does knowing what God says in His Word help you to transform your thinking about your role as a wife?

But What If...?

*"A wife after God's own heart
seeks to help, follow, respect, and love her husband
with all her heart."*

But what if I'm married to a man who is not a Christian?

> What instructions does 1 Corinthians 7:10-16 have for you?

> How does 2 Peter 1:3 help you to keep on keeping on in your marriage situation?

But what if I'm married to a "passive" Christian?

> Scan quickly through the sad story of Rebekah in Genesis 27. Isaac was a man who whined, moped, and lacked the backbone of a good leader at times. What did Rebekah do when her husband failed to lead? And what were the consequences to her family?

> What principles can you draw from Rebekah's behavior as a wife?

Back to the Basics

> *"When the red flag starts waving in your marriage,*
> *it's time to revisit God's blueprint for a wife*
> *and refresh your commitment to follow it."*

How long have you been married? And what "season" of your marriage do you consider you and your husband to be in? Briefly describe a few of the seasons and cycles you've already passed through...and the one you are in.

Are there any evaluations and adjustments you need to make? Do you need to go back to God's unchanging basics? Make notes here, and remember—God's guidelines for you as a wife will never change. They make up His unchanging plan for you.

Making a Difference

*"Your commitment to follow God's plan
makes a difference in the atmosphere in your home
and improves the climate of your marriage."*

Here's a checklist for making the commitments that will make a difference.

- ✓ Have you stopped, prayed, and revisited God's blueprint for your marriage?

- ✓ Have you refreshed your commitment to actively follow God's plan for your role in your marriage?

If you are married to a man who is not a Christian or is a "passive" Christian, how do these possibilities encourage you to keep on following God's plan for you as a Christian wife?

Sanctification of the unbeliever—

Salvation of the unbeliever—

Spiritual life—

Spiritual growth—

"Two Are Better than One"

"When a wife faithfully follows God's plan,
the possibilities are spectacular...
and the blessings are unending and eternal."

Look now at Ecclesiastes 4:9-10 in your Bible. In your own words, what are the truths—and the blessings!—about marriage revealed in these verses?

In light of the blessings and benefits of working together, how would you rate you and your husband as a team? Do you consider yourself to be an excellent team player? Please explain, and then jot down one change you can make to better your teamwork.

Heart Response

*"There is no substitute for the help, compassion,
companionship, care, and strength that
bless a couple when they work together as a team."*

Think now about your marriage—about you and your
husband as a team. Then write out in 100 words or less
your commitment for bettering your working relationship
with him, and seal it with a time of prayer.

Little Things That Make a Big Difference

Look again at the section in your chapter entitled "Little Things That Make a Big Difference." Because working as a team really matters in your marriage, what one "little thing" can you do this week to improve the teamwork in your marriage? Write it here...and don't forget to note the fantastic results!

I will...

Thank You, God, for the following changes, blessings, and results...

3

ℒearning to ℭommunicate

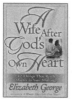 In your copy of *A Wife After God's Own Heart,* read the chapter entitled "Learning to Communicate." What meant the most to you as a married woman?

What offered you the greatest challenge as a wife?

What information was new or served as a fresh reminder for you as you seek to follow after God's own heart in your marriage?

Introductory Section

*"Every couple must learn how to communicate
so the needed adjustments in marriage
can be made more smoothly."*

In the length of time you've been a wife, what have you learned about the importance of communication in marriage? Share two lessons from your experience.

"Like Apples of Gold..."

"How can you and your husband work your way through emotions, disappointments, and confusion? The Bible tells you how."

Using the wording from your Bible, write out Proverbs 25:11:

As you seek "silver" and "golden" speech, note how God's formula will help in your communication with your husband. How can you apply the wisdom in the following verses to your marriage this week?

Soft (Proverbs 15:1 and Proverbs 25:15)—

Sweet (Proverbs 16:21)—

Suitable (Proverbs 16:24)—

Scant (Proverbs 10:19)—

Slow (James 1:19-20)—

"Like a Constant Dripping"

> *"God's Word gives you guidelines*
> *not only for your marriage*
> *but for your communication in marriage."*

What does each of these scriptures say about the effect a wife's words can have on her husband?

Proverbs 19:13—

Proverbs 21:9—

Proverbs 21:19—

Proverbs 27:15—

Now evaluate your speech patterns. Are any changes necessary? If so, what?

Performing Radical Surgery

"Pray for your words to minister to your husband and edify your relationship with him."

To turn a corner in your communication, do you need to...

> *Take it to the Lord in prayer?* Read about Hannah's situation in 1 Samuel 1:1-20. What do you learn about...
>
> ...living in a difficult marriage?
>
> ...the role of prayer in marriage difficulties?
>
> *Make a decision to "cut it out"?* Read Matthew 5:29-30. In what ways will radical surgery improve your communication according to...
>
> Proverbs 12:18—
>
> Proverbs 10:19—

Proceeding Ahead

*"Wise, godly speech and increased persuasiveness
is all about how you say what you say."*

As you consider the seven disciplines below, note how
you think each one would improve your communication
with your husband.

Learning to pray—

Learning to say nothing—

Learning to wait—

Learning to make a list—

Learning to make an appointment—

Learning to write it out—

Learning "to take the blame"—

Now star or circle the one you plan to work on.

Heart Response

*"A wife after God's own heart
asks Him for help with godly discipline over
the thoughts of her heart and
the words of her mouth."*

Think now about your marriage, especially about how you and your husband do—or don't—communicate. Then write out in 100 words or less your commitment to learn better ways of communicating with your husband, and seal it with a time of prayer.

Little Things That Make a Big Difference

Look again at the section in your chapter entitled "Little Things That Make a Big Difference." Because learning to communicate really matters in your marriage, what one "little thing" can you do this week to become a better communicator? Write it here...and don't forget to note the fantastic results!

I will...

Thank You, God, for the following changes, blessings, and results...

4

$\mathscr{E}$njoying $\mathscr{I}$ntimacy

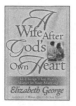

In your copy of *A Wife After God's Own Heart* read the chapter entitled "Enjoying Intimacy." What meant the most to you as a married woman?

What offered you the greatest challenge as a wife?

What information was new or served as a fresh reminder for you as you seek to follow after God's own heart in your marriage?

Created for Intimacy

"In the perfect environment, God's perfect couple
enjoyed a perfect existence
...and perfect intimacy."

Read the account of God's creation of Eve in Genesis
2:15-25. Pick out and record the words that reveal God's
intention for the first newly married couple's relationship.

According to Genesis 2:24, what two steps must a couple
take for intimacy to have its full effect?

Which has been the greater challenge in your marriage—
leaving or cleaving? Share why, and then jot down several
things you can do immediately to improve this area of
your marriage.

But...What Happened?

> *"Intimacy has been a struggle for all couples*
> *since the day Adam and Eve chose*
> *to listen to others instead of to God."*

Describe in your own words what happened in Genesis 3:1-6.

How did the serpent seduce Eve through...

      ...her appetites?

      ...her eyes?

      ...her pride?

What results occurred that marred the perfect and blissful intimacy Adam and Eve had enjoyed?

What warnings does Eve's "fall" into sin send to your heart?

Rekindling Intimacy

*"Your greatest progress and victory in intimacy
will be made as you choose to
view, perceive, and think about sex as God does."*

Look again at the six why's and how's regarding sexual intimacy in marriage. In what ways will these views help a married woman with her thinking and her approach to intimacy in her marriage?

Proclaimed (Genesis 2:24-25)—

Procreation (Genesis 1:27-28)—

Pleasure (Proverbs 5:15-19)—

Purity (1 Corinthians 7:2)—

Partnership (1 Corinthians 7:3-4)—

Protective (1 Corinthians 7:5)—

Was there a main message to your heart? Can you share it?

Giving Your All

> *"Sexual pleasure in marriage is God's will,*
> *God's plan, and God's gift to both partners.*
> *Therefore determine to give intimacy your all."*

How can these verses help you or any married woman...

...battle shyness—Genesis 2:24-25; Proverbs 5:19?

...remember that sex in marriage is honor-able—Hebrews 13:4?

...delight in giving and receiving sexual plea-sure—Proverbs 5:15-19?

...keep you from withholding sex from your husband—1 Corinthians 7:3-5?

Turning a Corner

*"When it comes to the sexual side of your marriage,
you are to give your all...
freely, unashamedly, joyfully, heartily, regularly."*

Of course you'll want to pray about giving your all to your husband in the Intimacy Department. And of course you'll want to talk to your husband. But in addition to talking to God and talking to your husband, you can do a few things to turn a corner and better your sexual relationship. From the following list, choose two to work on now. Then, as you progress, work your way through the other suggestions.

What Would Improve Your Sexual Relations?[1]

Gentle initiation	Better communication
Increased frequency	Better hygiene
Increased touching	Increased passion
More romance	Romantic atmosphere
Longer foreplay	Increased patience
More variety	Different time of day

Trusting God

> *"As you turn a corner and move out*
> *in response to God and to His Word,*
> *you will have to trust Him.*
> *This is a giant step of faith."*

What can you—or any wife—do to strengthen your faith and trust in God? Note at least three things that will help you start trusting God in the vital area of intimacy in your marriage.

Heart Response

*"Ask God to dispel any thoughts that oppose
His teaching regarding
the right, privilege, and enjoyment He intended
sex to bring to both you and your husband."*

Think now about your marriage—especially the area of intimacy in your relationship with your husband. Then write out in 100 words or less your commitment to trust God, to turn a corner, and to enjoy intimacy even more, and seal it with a time of prayer.

Little Things That Make a Big Difference

Look again at the section in your chapter entitled "Little Things That Make a Big Difference." Because sexual intimacy really matters in your marriage, what one "little thing" can you do this week to increase and improve the intimacy in your marriage? Write it here...and don't forget to note the fantastic results!

I will...

Thank You, God, for the following changes, blessings, and results...

5

Managing Your Money

In your copy of *A Wife After God's Own Heart,* read the chapter entitled "Managing Your Money." What meant the most to you as a married woman?

What offered you the greatest challenge as a wife?

What information was new or served as a fresh reminder for you as you seek to follow after God's own heart in your marriage?

Money Matters to God

*"Not only is money important to a married couple,
but it matters to God."*

Look at each of the following scriptures in your Bible.
How do these truths concerning your finances as a couple
encourage or instruct you?

Money is to be earned.

Genesis 3:17-19—

Proverbs 10:4—

Proverbs 13:11—

Proverbs 28:19—

How do these truths change your respect and support for your husband's efforts and time spent on
his job?

Money is to be given.

Deuteronomy 8:18—

1 Corinthians 16:1-2—

2 Corinthians 9:5-7—

Proverbs 31:20—

How do these truths change or strengthen your views about regularly giving a portion of your income as a couple?

And what is the promise of Luke 6:38?

Money is to be managed and saved.

> Proverbs 24:3-4—

> Proverbs 27:23-27—

> How do these truths spotlight the importance of being a wise and frugal manager of your resources?

Money is not to be desired.

> 1 Timothy 6:18—

> Proverbs 16:8—

> Proverbs 15:16—

> 1 Timothy 6:11—

> 1 Timothy 6:6-7—

> As you consider your heart—the heart of a woman after God's own heart—how do these truths speak to you?

Money Matters in Marriage

"Your family unit, your character, and your enterprises
will be blessed as you manage and save money
for the good of your loved ones."

Read Proverbs 31:10-31, and list at least five ways the "virtuous wife" contributed financially to her marriage.

—

—

—

—

—

What ideas can you take away from this passage that will help you be a more faithful steward of your joint income and assets (see especially verse 11)?

Money Should Matter to You

*"Managing God's money is not only a spiritual issue
requiring spiritual disciplines and character qualities,
but it is a matter of obedience."*

Wise money management and family finances most definitely involve you, the wife, in your household. How do you think the following practices will help you do a better job with God's resources?

Praying—

Giving—

Saving—

Budgeting—

Doing without—

Bewaring—

Growing in contentment—

Did you discover any weak areas? If so circle, star, or underline them, place them on your prayer list, talk them over with your husband, and set to work managing your money...God's way!

Mastering Your Money

"Master your money or it will master you!"

Read 1 Timothy 6:10. Now look at your checkbook and credit card statements and then answer this question: "Am I the master of my money, or is it mastering me?" What does your answer indicate?

Read Proverbs 3:9-10. How can you implement the following steps into your marriage...and your heart?

Present to God the firstfruits of all your income—

Put those communication skills to work and talk to your husband—

Put some personal goals into motion and make some personal changes—

Purchase a book about the financial in's and out's of home management—

Doing Your Part

> *"You contribute much to your husband*
> *by the wise, thrifty, diligent management*
> *and oversight of your part*
> *of the household budget."*

List a few of the things you are presently doing to con-tribute to the managing of the finances in your marriage.

After reading this section of your chapter, are there any additional ways you can help in the Money Department? How can you encourage your husband and support his efforts toward the financial well-being of your marriage?

$\mathcal{H}$eart $\mathcal{R}$esponse

*"You as a godly wife are
better than money to your husband!
'A virtuous wife' is far above rubies!"*

Think now about your marriage—especially the role finances play in your relationship with your husband. Then write out in 100 words or less your commitment to help your husband in every possible way with better money management, and seal it with a time of prayer.

Little Things That Make a Big Difference

Look again at the section in your chapter entitled "Little Things That Make a Big Difference." Because "money matters" really matters in your marriage, what one "little thing" can you do this week to help out with the household finances? Write it here...and don't forget to note the fantastic results!

I will...

Thank You, God, for the following changes, blessings, and results...

6

Keeping Up the Home

 In your copy of *A Wife After God's Own Heart,* read the chapter entitled "Keeping Up the Home." What meant the most to you as a married woman?

What offered you the greatest challenge as a wife?

What information was new or served as a fresh reminder for you as you seek to follow after God's own heart in your marriage?

God's Perspective on a Home

"Your home is important,
not only to you and your husband and children,
but to God."

Because your home matters to God, He has much to say about it in His Word. Look now at these verses in your "Homemaking Handbook"—your Bible—and discover God's perspective on a home.

You are to "build" your home.

> Look now at the following verses and note their message to your heart regarding "building" your home.
>
> Proverbs 9:1—
>
> Proverbs 14:1—
>
> Proverbs 24:3—
>
> Now look again at Proverbs 14:1, paying close attention to its final words. While the wise woman concentrates on building her home, what does the foolish woman do instead?
>
> In your chapter you were asked, "Are you building up your home...or are you breaking it down?" What evidence is available for either answer based on this past week?

You are to watch over your home.

Look now at the following verses, and note their message to your heart regarding "watching" over your home.

Proverbs 27:23—

Proverbs 31:27—

Now look again at Proverbs 31:27, paying close attention to its final words. How is the wise woman able to successfully watch over her home?

What further instruction and insight do these scriptures give?

Proverbs 14:23—

Proverbs 19:15—

As you think about these bits of divine wisdom, what can you—or any woman—do immediately to become a better home-watcher?

You are to manage your home.

> To better understand the message of 1 Timothy
> 5:13-14, read verses 3-14. As you think about
> your life as a married woman, can you point to
> some specific ways having a home to manage has
> caused you to mature? To become more respon-
> sible?

> Scan through Proverbs 31:10-31, and note some
> of the many ways this noble wife managed her
> home.

You are to keep your home.

> Read Titus 2:5 in your Bible, and describe what you believe it means to be a "worker at home" (NASB). Does your Bible translation use other words to describe this aspect of keeping up your home? If so, what does it say?

> Look also at these other scriptures that teach the principle of keeping up your home. What does each one add to your understanding of "home" making?

> Proverbs 7:11-12—

> Proverbs 14:1—

> 1 Timothy 5:13-14—

> What evidence is there from your homemaking efforts this past week that would indicate that your eye is focused on the place where you and your husband live? And what one change will you make for next week?

Problems and Solutions

> *"Something is always better than nothing…*
> *no matter how small that 'something' is!"*

Circle the problems you are plagued with in keeping up and improving your home. Then reread the solution for those problems in your book. Follow up by writing out several solutions to your dilemmas. For additional insights write out solutions to all of the problem situations below. You never know when you might be able to share what you know with another woman!

I'm so tired!

Solutions—

I have so many children!

Solutions—

I don't know what to do!

Solutions—

I don't know how!

    Solutions—

I don't care!

    Solutions—

I have a job!

    Solutions—(See Chapter 9.)

If you circled more than one problem, don't be discouraged. At some time, any and all-of-the-above are true of most every homemaker. Remember—A problem defined is a problem half solved. So start by praying over this list. Then talk with your husband. Together come up with the Number One problem from the list and with God's help seek a solution. Then go on to the next problem and move through the same exercise. Realize that management skills can be learned. Also know that there is no better place or way you can spend the precious time God gives you than by working out His will right under your own roof by your loving efforts put forth in keeping up your home for you and your husband!

*"If you have acquired some measure
of knowledge and skill
in any problem areas that a woman faces,
please make yourself available to your
struggling sisters."*

Think now about your marriage—especially the role your home and homemaking plays in your relationship with your husband. Then write out in 100 words or less your commitment to increase your efforts in keeping up your home, and seal it with a time of prayer.

Little Things That Make a Big Difference

Look again at the section in your chapter entitled "Little Things That Make a Big Difference." Because the place where you live really matters in your marriage, what one "little thing" can you do this week to improve where you and your husband forge your relationship—your home-sweet-home? Write it here...and don't forget to note the fantastic results!

I will...

Thank You, God, for the following changes, blessings, and results...

7

Raising Your Children

In your copy of *A Wife After God's Own Heart*, read the chapter entitled "Raising Your Children." What meant the most to you as a married woman and a mother?

What offered you the greatest challenge as a wife?

What information was new or served as a fresh reminder for you as you seek to follow after God's own heart in your marriage and family?

Parenting 101

*"God is giving you an assignment like no other.
While specific techniques for child-raising
will come, go, and change, there are certain core
values and fundamental practices that won't."*

Wherever you find yourself in the natural progression of marriage, family, and child-raising, know that God is at work in your life. Acknowledge and believe, too, that God desires to use you to raise your children to love and serve Him. As you work your way through the parenting exercises realize that parenting children places tremendous stress on most marriages. So beware!....And prepare to put the principles about how to have a great marriage to work overtime.

Following these few instructions will help you make the most of the biblical principles and the parenting phases addressed in the questions that follow.

—Read every referenced scripture in your Bible.

—Review all the guidelines even though you may presently fit into only one or two of the stages.

—Resolve to fulfill God's will for your life in your present parenting stage.

—Reflect back on the stages you have passed through.

—Remind yourself of God's grace during each of those stages.

—Renew your commitment to fulfill those guidelines that are yet future.

1. *Desire them*—What does the Bible teach you about desiring children?

    Genesis 1:28—

    Psalm 113:9—

    Psalm 127:3,5—

2. *Pray to have them*—What does Hannah teach you about praying to have children?

    1 Samuel 1:10-11—

3. *Welcome them*—What does Sarah teach you about the joy of welcoming children?

    Genesis 18:9-12—

    Genesis 21:1-6—

4. *Take them to church*—What do these scriptures
   teach you about taking your children to worship?

   Luke 2:21-22—

   Luke 2:41-42—

   Hebrews 10:24-25—

5. *Love them*—What do these scriptures teach you
   about loving and taking care of your children?

   Proverbs 31:14,15,21—

   Titus 2:4—

6. *Teach them*—What do these scriptures say about
   teaching God's Word to your children?

   Deuteronomy 6:6-7—

   2 Timothy 3:14-15—

7. *Train them*—What do these scriptures teach you about the importance of training your children?

>   Proverbs 1:8 and 6:20—

>   Proverbs 22:6—

>   Proverbs 31:1—

8. *Guide them*—How did these parents guide their children as the years passed by?

>   Judges 14:1-3—

>   Proverbs 31:1-9—

9. *Befriend them*—What do these scriptures teach you about being a good friend?

>   Proverbs 17:17—

>   Proverbs 18:24—

10. *Mates? Welcome them!*—What does this scripture teach you about your children's marriage partners?

   Genesis 2:24—

11. *Grandchildren? Welcome them!*—What does the heart of Naomi teach you about welcoming grandchildren?

   Ruth 4:16—

12. *Pray for them*—What do these scriptures teach you about the heart that prays?

   How are you to pray according to...

   ...James 5:16?

   How often are you to pray according to...

   ...Ephesians 6:18?

   ...1 Thessalonians 5:17?

   What are you to pray for your children? For a sample, see—and pray!—Colossians 1:9-14 on behalf of your children, their mates, and their children.

Now that you know the scriptural guidelines that make up Parenting 101, take the next step to grow in your role as a mother and in your child-raising efforts. For each guideline that applies to you, note one action you will take to be a mother after God's own heart.

1. Desire them—

2. Pray to have them—

3. Welcome them—

4. Take them to church—

5. Love them—

6. Teach them—

7. Train them—

8. Guide them—

9. Befriend them—

10. Mates? Welcome them!—

11. Grandchildren? Welcome them!—

12. Pray for them—

Heart Response

*"Any Christian woman who has
children, stepchildren, or grandchildren has
an important duty and responsibility before God
concerning those children He has placed in her life."*

Think now about your marriage—especially the roles your children (or potential children) and your parenting play in your life as a wife and as a mother. Then write out in 100 words or less your commitment to increase your efforts in godly parenting, and seal it with a time of prayer.

Little Things That Make a Big Difference

Look again at the section in your chapter entitled "Little Things That Make a Big Difference." Because your efforts at raising your children really matters in your marriage, what one "little thing" can you do this week to be a better mother after God's own heart? Write it here...and don't forget to note the fantastic results!

I will...

Thank You, God, for the following changes, blessings, and results...

8

Extending Love to Family

 In your copy of *A Wife After God's Own Heart,* read the chapter entitled "Extending Love to Family." What meant the most to you as a married woman?

What offered you the greatest challenge as a wife?

What information was new or served as a fresh reminder for you as you seek to follow after God's own heart in your marriage?

God's Perfect Plan

> *"Through marriage, God makes each*
> *family become two—*
> *two units that are friends and dedicated*
> *to one another, two units that love and cherish*
> *one another and gladly invite*
> *the other into their hearts."*

What do you think are some of the most common sources of conflict between a couple and their parents?

What are some things couples do to exclude their parents from their lives in casual or even hurtful, disrespectful ways?

The First Law with a Promise

> *"God asks for obedience to His command*
> *to honor parents, and He promises*
> *a spiritually blessed life on the way*
> *to the higher blessing of eternal life."*

Read Exodus 20:12 and Ephesians 6:2-3 in your Bible. Look up the word "honor" in a dictionary, and write out the definition.

What are some ways you have shown honor to your parents and your husband's parents?

Now think of some practical ways you can enhance and strengthen your relationships with your parents and your in-laws in the present.

Love Lived Out

> *"You are on a mission to learn to love,*
> *cherish, honor, and respect your family members.*
> *This includes your mother-in-law!"*

As a prelude to examining the lives of two remarkable, biblical women, it will be well worth your time to read the short book of Ruth in your Bible. It will probably take you less than ten minutes. It is from Ruth and Naomi that we will learn the following principles for extending love to family.

Ruth respected her mother-in-law.

> Read Ruth 1:16-17 in your Bible. Then plan a time to follow through on the exercises suggested for your parents and your husband's, too. But for now, take the time to write out the exercise on the next two pages.

Ten Things I Appreciate About
My Mother-in-Law

1.

2.

3.

4.

5.

6.

7.

8.

9.

10.

Ruth was loyal to her mother-in-law.

For a picture of loyalty, read Ruth 1:8-13,16-17 in your Bible. Then look at the verses that follow, and note what they teach about the words that come out of your mouth.

Ephesians 4:29,31-32—

Titus 3:2—

And how about your heart? In Luke 6:45, what did Jesus say about its connection to the words you speak?

Now analyze your speech patterns with and about your extended family in light of loyalty. Are there any changes you need to make in your speech? In your heart? Note them here.

What will you do the next time someone in your family (even you!) wants to talk negatively about another family member?

Ruth wanted to be with her mother-in-law.

> Think about this: Do you enjoy being with your mother and mother-in-law? Why or why not?

> If your times with family are not enjoyable, what steps can *you* take to turn things around? (And please notice the word *you!* If your family members are the problem, only God can change them. But make sure *your* heart is right and open to being a peacemaker.) Make a to-do list here and now. Then place several of the steps on your calendar or planner and follow through.

Ruth served her mother-in-law.

> Read Ruth 2:2-18. First think of the hottest, dustiest, driest day you have ever experienced. That's the kind of day it was when Ruth volunteered to serve her mother-in-law...outside! Then jot down a list of the things—both big and little—Ruth did to serve her mother-in-law and care for her needs.

> What are some things—both big and little—you can do to serve your parents and in-laws? Again, place several of them on your calendar or planner and follow through.

Ruth took her mother-in-law's advice.

> *"I hope and pray you are a wife who seeks,*
> *listens to, and follows any godly, practical advice*
> *your elders pass on to you. Wisdom listens!"*

Have your parents or in-laws ever given you unsolicited advice? If so, how did you respond?

Now look at these verses from Proverbs, and write them out. Then circle the two types of people contrasted in each verse.

Proverbs 12:15—

Proverbs 15:5—

Proverbs 23:9—

How should you respond to advice according to these words of wisdom?

Ruth blessed her mother-in-law.

> Read Ruth 4:13-16. In how many ways do you notice Ruth bringing joy to her mother-in-law?

Ruth let her mother-in-law help her.

> Review Ruth 4:13-16 again. In what one major way do you notice Ruth allowing her mother-in-law to help her?

Are you a Ruth? A young married or a young mom with a baby or two? What do you normally say to your mother and mother-in-law when they offer to help out in some way? Are there any reasons why you shouldn't let them help? If you've somehow sent out an erroneous message that you don't need or desire their help, what can you ask them to do that includes them in your family circle? Pray for you? Babysit for an hour? Give you instruction on a cleaning project? Give you advice on a menu or recipe? Loan you something—a vacuum cleaner if yours is broken or extra dishes for entertaining? Be creative, but think of something, even if they live across the continent. They would probably both love to help, and are just waiting to be invited! You honor your mother and mother-in-law by asking for help!

Are you a Naomi? The older, wiser, experienced woman? If so, what are you doing to offer help to your married children? I recently heard a young mother relate that her parents said they would come from out of town to visit them on one condition—if they were not asked to do anything or help in any way, especially babysit their grandchildren. Hopefully this is not your attitude if you are a grandmother. What a privilege it is to assist your children and to spend time with your grandchildren—to have input into the future of your family!

*H*eart *R*esponse

*"You and I have no excuses
for not bettering our family relationships."*

Think now about your marriage—especially the roles
your relationships with your parents and in-laws play in
your life as a wife. Then write out in 100 words or less
your commitment to extend love to all your family members, and seal it with a time of prayer.

Little Things That Make a Big Difference

Look again at the section in your chapter entitled "Little Things That Make a Big Difference." Because your family, your husband's family, and your extended family really matters in your marriage, what one "little thing" can you do this week to improve those relationships? Write it here...and don't forget to note the fantastic results!

I will...

Thank You, God, for the following changes, blessings, and results...

9

Tending Your Career

 In your copy of *A Wife After God's Own Heart,* read the chapter entitled "Tending Your Career." What meant the most to you as a married woman?

What offered you the greatest challenge as a wife?

What information was new or served as a fresh reminder for you as you seek to follow after God's own heart in your marriage?

Doing God's Will

> *"What is a woman after God's own heart?*
> *She is a woman who seeks with all her heart*
> *to fulfill God's will."*

Look first at Acts 13:22 in your Bible, and write it out here.

Look next at each of the scriptures below that represent a wife after God's own heart's major priorities. Jot down their messages to your heart.

Love God (Matthew 22:37-38)—

Love her husband (Titus 2:4)—

Love her children (Titus 2:4)—

Love her home (Titus 2:5)—

Love and serve God's people
(1 Corinthians 12:4-7)—

Are there any adjustments that need to be made in your priorities? Or, to put it another way, Where is the focus of your life, heart, and time?

*"How does a woman with a 9 A.M. to 5 P.M. job
keep her priorities in order?"*

Whether you are presently working outside the home or
not, answering these questions will be beneficial for you.
It will help your understanding of why you are in the
workplace and/or help you counsel other women.

1. *Why am I working?*

   List the reasons you are working outside the home.
   Be honest because your answers to this question will
   help clarify your motives.

2. *Have I explained my desires and concerns to my husband?*

   Learn now from Nehemiah and Esther, two of God's people who needed to ask something of their respective kings.

   > *Nehemiah*—What was the problem (Nehemiah 1:3)?

   > How did Nehemiah respond to the problem (verses 4-11)?

   > *Esther*—What was the problem (Esther 3:8-9)?

   > How did Esther respond to the problem (4:16–5:4)?

   What lessons can you learn from Nehemiah and Esther about approaching your husband?

3. *Have I properly researched my options?*

Today there are a multitude of options to the "traditional job." Can you think of a few? Be sure to look carefully at the many ways the industrious woman in Proverbs 31:10-31 contributed to her household finances...from home! Then, if staying home is important to you, what steps can you take this week to research this option?

4. *Do I have goals that will allow me to quit working?*

Do you desire to step down from full-time to part-time work or to stop working outside the home altogether? Set some goals with your husband. What immediate steps can you take to begin the process? How long will the process take? And how does the truth of Proverbs 21:5 encourage you in your planning process?

5. *What can (or must) be eliminated from my life?*

If quitting work is not an option for you, look again at your God-given priorities listed at the beginning of this lesson. Jot down below any activities and pursuits that fall outside of these priority areas. Prayerfully consider eliminating as many of these nonpriority involvements as possible. Which nonpriority activity will be the first to go? How does the principle of "little" things in Song of Solomon 2:15 encourage you in your planning process?

6. *How can I do a better job of managing my time?*

What home duties can you delegate to your children? To your husband? What errands can you take care of on the way to work? On your lunch hour? On the way home from work? Take control of your time, and watch the truth of Proverbs 21:5 become a reality!

7. *Am I neglecting my relationship with the Lord?*

Due to the busyness of life, what spiritual disciplines have been neglected in your relationship with the Lord? How will eliminating nonpriority activities (see Question 5) help restore that relationship? Can you think of any other ways to make Matthew 6:33 a reality in your daily life?

8. *Is my perspective right?*

"True fulfillment comes from the strong and lasting relationships you are building right under your own roof. Family lasts a lifetime—a job does not." How strongly do you believe this statement? And how does Proverbs 31:12,27-31 help with your perspective?

9. *Am I diligently and fervently praying for God to work in my husband's heart?*

   On a separate sheet of paper, write out a prayer to God for your husband. Include his spiritual condition. His work. His time or lack of time with the children. His relationship with you, and your relationship with him. His attitude about your working. Add anything else that might be unique to your marriage. Then pray this prayer every day. And while you are praying, don't forget to ask God for His grace to sustain you in your many responsibilities—especially in your role as a wife!

10. *Am I faithfully endeavoring to follow God's priorities for my life?*

   Once again, list your God-given priorities. In one sentence, state what one large new thing you will do to endeavor to follow God's priorities for your life.

Heart Response

"Where is your heart?
Is it at home, at your home-sweet-home?
Every woman, and perhaps especially
the woman who tends a career,
must ask and answer this question every day."

Think now about your marriage—especially the role knowing and practicing your priorities plays in your life as a wife. Then write out in 100 words or less your commitment to keep God's priorities in mind, whether you work or not, and seal it with a time of prayer.

Little Things That Make a Big Difference

Look again at the section in your chapter entitled "Little Things That Make a Big Difference." Because your efforts at home and in your relationships really matter in your marriage, what one "little thing" can you do this week to bring better balance to your responsibilities, especially if you are juggling your "job" at home and an "outside" job? Write it here...and don't forget to note the fantastic results!

I will...

Thank You, God, for the following changes, blessings, and results...

10

Making Time for Fun

 In your copy of *A Wife After God's Own Heart,* read the chapter entitled "Making Time for Fun." What meant the most to you as a married woman?

What offered you the greatest challenge as a wife?

What information was new or served as a fresh reminder for you as you seek to follow after God's own heart in your marriage?

How Did It All Begin?

> *"Recalling the memories of the playful pleasures*
> *you once enjoyed will be the spark*
> *that ignites more fun in your day today."*

It's your turn to take a few minutes and jot down several recollections about how you and your husband met, about how it all began between the two of you. Describe…

…the first time you met—

…the first time you talked at length—

…the first crazy thing the two of you did together—

…the scene of his proposal—

What were the things about him that stood out most?

What were some of the fun things you did back in your courtship and honeymoon days?

But...What Happened to the Fun?

"If you're like most couples,
real life sets in all too soon.
Reality can begin to nibble away at the fun that
was unique to you and your husband."

The following is a list of culprits that can rob you of fun in your marriage. As you work your way through these joy-robbers, write down at least one step you could take in each area. Also, as you consider each challenge to a happy marriage, note what advice you would give to other couples.

Responsibility—How can the soberness of life over-shadow the joy and fun that should be in your marriage?

Money matters—How can the lack of money affect your thinking about fun in your marriage?

Children—How can the arrival of children and the resulting constant care pull at a couple's time and relationship?

Exhaustion—How can a steady diet of tiredness steal away the energy needed to spark a little couple fun?

Discouragement—How can the emotions and tiredness generated by stress, difficulties, and obstacles lead to a lack of fun in a husband–wife relationship?

Recapturing the Fun

"Realize that the ultimate source of all joy is the Lord.
If you belong to God through His Son Jesus Christ,
yours is the deepest, purest, fullest joy
that any person can possess."

As you set about to curb the robbers of the joy God meant for you and your husband to revel in, pay special attention to these truths about joy. After looking at each verse in your Bible, write down its message to your heart...and marriage.

Joy must begin in your heart.

Proverbs 15:13—

Joy's ultimate source is the Lord.

Nehemiah 8:10—

Psalm 5:11—

Galatians 5:22—

Joy can be purposefully cultivated. Note what each verse teaches about joy.

☞   Purposefully rejoice each day.

.   Psalm 118:24—

Philippians 4:4—

What are you doing today to rejoice in the Lord?

☞   Purposefully play music.

Psalm 100:2—

Ephesians 5:19—

Colossians 3:16—

What music are you playing?

🐝 Purposefully put on a smile.

>   Proverbs 15:13—

>   Proverbs 15:30—

>   Have you smiled at your husband today?

Joy can result from your creativity.

>   Song of Solomon 2:10-13—

>   Song of Solomon 7:11-13—

>   What fun interlude have you planned lately?

Where Do I Start?

> *"Plan to have fun, make time for fun,
> have fun, and have a string of fun memories!"*

Look again at the suggestions given on where to start making time for fun. Have you tried any of these with your husband yet? If so, share your fun experience. (And note, none of these activities costs a cent! You're going to eat anyway, and most museums have a "free" day each month.)

Cook together?

Play a game together?

Tour a museum together?

Go downtown together?

Go to a park together?

Which one might be the easiest to get your husband involved in and why?

Which ones might be a little more challenging and why?

Now how about you? What fun activities can you think of?

Heart Response

*"It was of her husband, the person she walked and
visited and played with and had fun with,
that the wife in Song of Solomon said,
'This is my beloved, and this is my friend.'"*

Think now about your marriage—especially the role
having fun together plays in your life as a couple. Then
write out in 100 words or less your commitment to
increase your efforts in making time for fun, and seal it
with a time of prayer.

Little Things That Make a Big Difference

Look again at the section in your chapter entitled "Little Things That Make a Big Difference." Because having fun really matters in your marriage, what one "little thing" can you do this week to make time for fun with your husband? Write it here...and don't forget to note the fantastic results!

I will...

Thank You, God, for the following changes, blessings, and results...

11

Serving the Lord

 In your copy of *A Wife After God's Own Heart,* read the chapter entitled "Serving the Lord." What meant the most to you as a married woman?

What offered you the greatest challenge as a wife?

What information was new or served as a fresh reminder for you as you seek to follow after God's own heart in your marriage?

Serving as a Christian

We serve out of motivation.

Salvation is a wonderful gift provided for us by God through His Son, Jesus Christ. Once we embrace Him as our Lord and Savior, we instantly realize that we owe a debt we cannot pay. But we can each, out of pure gratitude, serve our Lord to our dying breath. Remind yourself of God's gift of salvation by looking up these verses and noting their truths.

John 3:3—

2 Corinthians 5:17—

Ephesians 2:4-5—

Colossians 1:12-14—

1 Peter 2:9—

How do these truths motivate you to serve the Lord?

We serve like Jesus, our model.

These verses point to how Jesus modeled a life of service. How do they relate to you?

John 5:30—

John 4:34—

Matthew 20:28—

Acts 10:38—

Next look up and note how we should model our Savior, even to the point of suffering.

1 Peter 2:21—

Are you serving in the way of the Master? Are you laboring on to the point of spending and being spent? Or are you languishing, absorbed in other pursuits, content to let others do the work of ministry? After searching your heart, note the direction your service needs to take.

We serve out our mandate.

What do these verses teach about your spiritual gifts?

 Romans 12:6—

 1 Corinthians 12:7—

 1 Timothy 4:14—

 2 Timothy 1:6—

Read through these passages and briefly list the spiritual gifts that were ministered in the Bible.

 Romans 12:6-8—

 1 Corinthians 12:8-10—

 1 Peter 4:9-11—

We serve as our ministry to others.

Do you know what your spiritual gift (or gifts) is? If so, write it down. If you're not quite sure what your gift(s) might be, answer the following questions:

> If you could do anything at your church, what would you like to do? (God has gifted you. His desires will be your desires—see Psalm 37:4.)

> What have you done that has blessed others? (When people share how you have blessed them with your ministry, they are indicating how God has used you as His gifted vessel in their lives.)

> What have you done in ministry that was a joy and seemed to be spiritually energized as you served? (Such ministry indicates the power of the Holy Spirit working through the spiritual gift God has given to you.)

> Ask others what they have observed as you have served. What gift(s) do they think you have? (Sometimes we cannot recognize our gifts...but others certainly can!)

We serve our Master.

What do these scriptures indicate about the Person you serve?

Matthew 25:35-40—

Acts 9:6—

Acts 27:23—

Colossians 3:24—

How are you to serve the Lord as taught in these verses?

Psalm 100:2—

Colossians 3:23—

How does the fact that you serve the Lord encourage you in your service?

Serving as a Couple

Serving as a couple may or may not be possible for you in your unique marital situation. If not, pray for God to open that door of ministry in the future. If so, realize that...

> *"Serving as a team will bring
> twice the love, twice the strength, and
> twice the service to those in need."*

Meet Sarah and Abraham.

Read Genesis 18:1-8 in your Bible.

Where did Sarah and Abraham reside?

Who were the visitors?

What was Abraham's immediate response?

What did Abraham offer his guests?

How did this couple work together as a team to provide hospitality to their three "heavenly visitors"?

How does this couple's use of their home inspire you to work with your husband to minister hospitality to others?

Meet Priscilla and Aquila.

Together Priscilla and Aquila worked as tentmakers, knew and shared the teachings of God's Word, opened their home to others, and encountered life-threatening persecution for their faith. What a couple! Briefly describe their ministry according to the following scriptures.

> Acts 18:1-3—Who was the recipient of this couple's ministry? What was their specific service in this instance?

> Acts 18:24-28—Who was the recipient of this couple's ministry? What was their specific service in this instance?

> 1 Corinthians 16:19—What ministry is evidenced here?

> Romans 16:3-5—List the variety of ministries referred to here about Priscilla and Aquila.

How does this couple's use of their knowledge, gifts, and home inspire you to work with your husband to minister to others?

Principles for a Wife's Ministry

> *"When the people and the place at home*
> *are taken care of, it is then that*
> *we take care of and tend to others."*

As you review the principles for a wife's ministry in your book, ask God to help you search your heart and evaluate your ministry, your motives, and your marriage.

1. *Serve those at home first*—Is your husband happy with the "service" he is receiving at home from a Spirit-filled wife? Is he receiving the firstfruits of your service...or does he feel like he is taking second place to the people at the church or elsewhere?

2. *Serve with your husband's blessing and support*— Have you stepped into a ministry without obtaining your husband's blessing and support? Did you forge ahead in a burst of enthusiasm...without even thinking of him or consulting him?

3. *Serve however you can*—There are many ministries that require only a servant's heart. How can you and your husband serve? If your husband has no desire to serve, how can you serve without neglecting or offending him?

Heart Response

*"Develop a servant's heart.
Every day of your God-given life
is to be a day of glorious service."*

Think now about your marriage—especially your roles of service at home as a wife and at church. Then write out in 100 words or less your commitment to increase your efforts toward greater service in both places, and seal it with a time of prayer.

Little Things That Make a Big Difference

Look again at the section in your chapter entitled "Little Things That Make a Big Difference." Because how and when you serve the Lord and His people really matters in your marriage, what one "little thing" can you do this week to be sensitive and balanced as a servant after God's own heart? Write it here...and don't forget to note the fantastic results!

I will...

Thank You, God, for the following changes, blessings, and results...

12

Reaching Out to Others

 In your copy of *A Wife After God's Own Heart,* read the chapter entitled "Reaching Out to Others." What meant the most to you as a married woman?

What offered you the greatest challenge as a wife?

What information was new or served as a fresh reminder for you as you seek to follow after God's own heart in your marriage?

Introductory Section

> *"You shall be witnesses to Me*
> *in Jerusalem, and in all Judea and Samaria,*
> *and to the end of the earth" (Acts 1:8).*

What is your story about how you heard about Jesus Christ? Who are the people who reached out to you? Take a few minutes to briefly write your story—to name names and to thank God in prayer for His Son and the people who shared His love with you. Then consider writing notes of gratitude to the people who brought the Good News to you.

Reaching Out to Your Husband

"Living a lovely life
preaches a louder and lovelier message
than your lips could ever proclaim."

Begin by reading 1 Peter 3:1-6 in your Bible and answering the following questions.

> What do verses 1-2 say about your behavior and conduct as a wife?

> What does verse 3 say about your appearance?

> What does verse 4 say about your heart?

> What do verses 5-6 say about your faith in God?

> What may be the result of such godly living in your husband's life (verse 1)?

Whether you are married to a believer or unbeliever, what do these verses teach you as a wife?

Reaching Out to Your Children

> *"We are to give our all each and every day*
> *to do our part to lead our little (and big!) ones*
> *to the knowledge of God and His Son Jesus Christ."*

Write out the message to you as a mother from each of these verses that speak to your responsibility to your children.

Deuteronomy 6:6-7—

Proverbs 22:6—

Ephesians 6:4—

Are you falling short in any of these fundamentals of Christian parenting? Are you failing to take the time these godly activities require? Do you need to make some changes in your daily schedule to allow time for any or all of the above? What can you do to improve in these areas?

Read through the list that follows and check those activities that you are presently pursuing with your children. Which unchecked box or boxes will you prayerfully start to incorporate into your parenting? Make a note of the first steps you will take in each activity.

❏ read the Bible regularly to them

❏ study the lives of God's great heroes of the faith with them

❏ have daily devotions with them

❏ help to hide God's Word in their hearts

❏ take them to church, Sunday school, and church activities

❏ speak of the Lord continually to them

❏ point the events of their lives to biblical truth

❏ pray for and with them at bedtime

❏ teach them about Jesus

❏ freely and frequently share God's plan of salvation

Reaching Out to Your Neighbors

> *"As you pray regularly for your neighbors,
> they come to have a place in your heart."*

What did Jesus say is to be the twofold focus of your love and attention?

Matthew 22:37-38—

Matthew 22:39—

What steps have you taken in the following areas to reach out to your neighbors? In what ways will you begin to reach out to your neighbors?

Prayer—

Hospitality—

Invitations to church activities—

Invitations to social events—

Reaching Out to Your Family

> *"A heart filled with God's love*
> *will smooth the way for reaching out to family—*
> *both your relatives and those of your husband."*

Count now, if you can, the number of people who make up your "family" beyond your husband, children, and grandchildren. Then add to that the number of people who make up your husband's family. What number did you come up with?

How does Romans 12:18 encourage you as you reach out to your family members?

How does the fact that Christ lives within you encourage you as you reach out to your family members (see Colossians 1:27)?

How does the knowledge of "the fruit of the Spirit" encourage you as you reach out to your family members (see Galatians 5:22-23)?

Now, do you agree or disagree that God can enable you to get along with any and all of your family members?

Reaching Out to the World

> *"Go therefore and make disciples*
> *of all the nations."*
> —Matthew 28:19

More than likely you will never be a missionary in a far-away country. But that shouldn't stop you from reaching out to the world in numerous ways. You can...

- ❦ Give of your finances to support missions.

- ❦ Pray for the missionaries your church supports.

- ❦ Invite missionaries into your home.

- ❦ Pick a country and pray for the salvation of its people.

- ❦ Go on a summer missions trip.

- ❦ Participate in your church's outreach projects.[1]

In your particular marital situation, which ones of these projects could you participate in to reach out to the world?

Reaching Out...Carefully!

"When it comes to reaching out to others
through your church, you want to serve
with your husband's blessing and support."

Look again at the three principles for a wife's ministry.
Are you reaching out carefully, honoring your husband's
wishes?

Heart Response

*"Has your faith in God been built up and
your commitment to be God's kind of wife firmed up?
Keep on keeping on as you travel the path of life
as a woman and a wife after God's own heart!"*

Think now about your marriage—especially in light of reaching out to others. Then write out in 100 words or less your commitment to increase your efforts in tending to your husband and reaching out to others, and seal it with a time of prayer.

Little Things That Make a Big Difference

Look again at the section in your chapter entitled "Little Things That Make a Big Difference." Because your efforts in reaching out to others really affects your marriage, what one "little thing" can you do this week to extend God's love to your husband and then to others? Write it here...and don't forget to note the fantastic results!

I will...

Thank You, God, for the following changes, blessings, and results...

Leading a Bible Study Discussion Group

What a privilege it is to lead a Bible study! And what joy and excitement await you as you delve into the Word of God and help others to discover its life-changing truths. If God has called you to lead a Bible study group, I know you'll be spending much time in prayer and planning and giving much thought to being an effective leader. I also know that taking the time to read through the following tips will help you to navigate the challenges of leading a Bible study discussion group and enjoying the effort and opportunity.

The Leader's Roles

As a Bible study group leader, you'll find your role changing back and forth from *expert* to *cheerleader* to *lover* to *referee* during the course of a session.

Since you're the leader, group members will look to you to be the *expert* guiding them through the material. So be well prepared. In fact, be over-prepared so that you know the material better than any group member does. Start your study early in the week and let its message simmer all week long. (You might even work several lessons ahead so that you have in mind the big picture and the overall direction of the study.) Be ready to share some additional gems that your group members wouldn't have discovered on their own. That extra insight from your study time— or that comment from a wise Bible teacher or scholar, that clever saying, that keen observation from another believer, and even an appropriate joke—adds an element of fun and keeps Bible study from becoming routine, monotonous, and dry.

Next, be ready to be the group's *cheerleader*. Your energy and enthusiasm for the task at hand can be contagious. It can also stimulate people to get more involved in their personal study as well as in the group discussion.

Third, be the *lover,* the one who shows a genuine concern for the members of the group. You're the one who will establish the atmosphere of the group. If you laugh and have fun, the group members will laugh and have fun. If you hug, they will hug. If you care, they will care. If you share, they will share. If you love, they will love. So pray every day to love the women God has placed in your group. Ask Him to show you how to love them with His love.

Finally, as the leader, you'll need to be the *referee* on occasion. That means making sure everyone has an equal opportunity to speak. That's easier to do when you operate under the assumption that every member of the group has something worthwhile to contribute. So, trusting that the Lord has taught each person during the week, act on that assumption.

Expert, cheerleader, lover, and referee—these four roles of the leader may make the task seem overwhelming. But that's not bad if it keeps you on your knees praying for your group.

A Good Start

Beginning on time, greeting people warmly, and opening in prayer gets the study off to a good start. Know what you want to have happen during your time together and make sure those things get done. That kind of order means comfort for those involved.

Establish a format and let the group members know what that format is. People appreciate being in a Bible study that focuses on the Bible. So keep the discussion on the topic and move the group through the questions. Tangents are often hard to avoid—and even harder to rein in. So be sure to focus on the answers to questions about the specific passage at hand. After all, the purpose of the group is Bible study!

Finally, as someone has accurately observed, "Personal growth is one of the by-products of any effective small group. This growth is achieved when people are recognized and accepted by others. The more friendliness, mutual trust, respect, and warmth exhibited, the more likely that the member will find pleasure in the group, and, too, the more likely she will work hard toward the accomplishment of the group's goals. The effective leader will strive to reinforce desirable traits" (source unknown).

A Dozen Helpful Tips

Here is a list of helpful suggestions for leading a Bible study discussion group:

1. Arrive early, ready to focus fully on others and give of yourself. If you have to do any last-minute preparation, review, re-grouping, or praying, do it in the car. Don't dash in, breathless, harried, late, still tweaking your plans.

2. Check out your meeting place in advance. Do you have everything you need—tables, enough chairs, a blackboard, hymnals if you plan to sing, coffee, etc.?

3. Greet each person warmly by name as she arrives. After all, you've been praying for these women all week long, so let each VIP know that you're glad she's arrived.

4. Use name tags for at least the first two or three weeks.

5. Start on time no matter what—even if only one person is there!

6. Develop a pleasant but firm opening statement. You might say, "This lesson was great! Let's get started so we can enjoy all of it!" or "Let's pray before we begin our lesson."

7. Read the questions, but don't hesitate to reword them on occasion. Rather than reading an entire paragraph of instructions, for instance, you might say, "Question 1 asks us to list some ways that Christ

displayed humility. Lisa, please share one way Christ displayed humility."

8. Summarize or paraphrase the answers given. Doing so will keep the discussion focused on the topic, eliminate digressions, help avoid or clear up any misunderstandings of the text, and keep each group member aware of what the others are saying.

9. Keep moving and don't add any of your own questions to the discussion time. It's important to get through the study guide questions. So if a cut-and-dried answer is called for, you don't need to comment with anything other than a "thank you." But when the question asks for an opinion or an application (for instance, "How can this truth help us in our marriages?" or "How do *you* find time for your quiet time?"), let all who want to contribute do so.

10. Affirm each person who contributes, especially if the contribution was very personal, painful to share, or a quiet person's rare statement. Make everyone who shares a hero by saying something like "Thank you for sharing that insight from your own life," or "We certainly appreciate what God has taught you. Thank you for letting us in on it."

11. Watch your watch, put a clock right in front of you, or consider using a timer. Pace the discussion so that you meet your cut-off time, especially if you want time to pray. Stop at the designated time even if you haven't finished the lesson. Remember that everyone has

worked through the study once; you are simply going over it again.

12. End on time. You can only make friends with your group members by ending on time or even a little early! Besides, members of your group have the next item on their agenda to attend to—picking up children from the nursery, babysitter, or school; heading home to tend to matters there; running errands; getting to bed; or spending some time with their husbands. So let them out *on time!*

Five Common Problems

In any group, you can anticipate certain problems. Here are some common ones that can arise, along with helpful solutions:

1. *The incomplete lesson*—Right from the start, establish the policy that if someone has not done the lesson, it is best for her not to answer the questions. But do try to include her responses to questions that ask for opinions or experiences. Everyone can share some thoughts in reply to a question like, "Reflect on what you know about both athletic and spiritual training and then share what you consider to be the essential elements of training oneself in godliness."

2. *The gossip*—The Bible clearly states that gossiping is wrong, so you don't want to allow it in your group. Set a high and strict standard by saying, "I am not

comfortable with this conversation," or "We [not *you*] are gossiping, ladies. Let's move on."

3. *The talkative member*—Here are three scenarios and some possible solutions for each.

a. The problem talker may be talking because she has done her homework and is excited about something she has to share. She may also know more about the subject than the others and, if you cut her off, the rest of the group may suffer.

   SOLUTION: Respond with a comment like: "Sarah, you are making very valuable contributions. Let's see if we can get some reactions from the others," or "I know Sarah can answer this. She's really done her homework. How about some of the rest of you?"

b. The talkative member may be talking because she has *not* done her homework and wants to contribute, but she has no boundaries.

   SOLUTION: Establish at the first meeting that those who have not done the lesson do not contribute except on opinion or application questions. You may need to repeat this guideline at the beginning of each session.

c. The talkative member may want to be heard whether or not she has anything worthwhile to contribute.

SOLUTION: After subtle reminders, be more direct, saying, "Betty, I know you would like to share your ideas, but let's give others a chance. I'll call on you later."

4. *The quiet member*—Here are two scenarios and possible solutions.

   a. The quiet member wants the floor but somehow can't get the chance to share.

   SOLUTION: Clear the path for the quiet member by first watching for clues that she wants to speak (moving to the edge of her seat, looking as if she wants to speak, perhaps even starting to say something) and then saying, "Just a second. I think Chris wants to say something." Then, of course, make her a hero!

   b. The quiet member simply doesn't want the floor.

   SOLUTION: "Chris, what answer do you have on question 2?" or "Chris, what do you think about...?" Usually after a shy person has contributed a few times, she will become more confident and more ready to share. Your role is to provide an opportunity where there is *no* risk of a wrong answer. But occasionally a group member will tell you that she would rather not be called on. Honor her request, but from time to time ask her privately if she feels ready to contribute to the group discussions.

   In fact, give all your group members the right to pass. During your first meeting, explain that any time a group member does not care to share an answer, she may simply say, "I pass." You'll want to repeat this policy at the beginning of every group session.

5. *The wrong answer*—Never tell a group member that she has given a wrong answer, but at the same time never let a wrong answer go by.

SOLUTION: Either ask if someone else has a different answer or ask additional questions that will cause the right answer to emerge. As the women get closer to the right answer, say, "We're getting warmer! Keep thinking! We're almost there!"

Learning from Experience

Immediately after each Bible study session, evaluate the group discussion time using this checklist. You may also want a member of your group (or an assistant or trainee or outside observer) to evaluate you periodically. May God strengthen—and encourage!—you as you assist others in the discovery of His many wonderful truths.

$\mathcal{N}$otes

Chapter 4

1.   Steve Stephens from *Understanding the One You Love* quoted in Alice Gray, *Lists to Live By for Every Married Couple* (Sisters, OR: Multnomah Publishers, 2001), pp. 86-87.

Chapter 12

1.   Adapted from Jim George, *A Husband After God's Own Heart* (Eugene, OR: Harvest House Publishers, 2004), p. 207.

Personal Notes

Personal Notes

Personal Notes

Personal Notes

Personal Notes

Personal Notes

Personal Notes

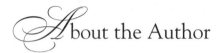

About the Author

Elizabeth George is a bestselling author and speaker whose passion is to teach the Bible in a way that changes women's lives. For information about Elizabeth's books or speaking ministry, to sign up for her mailings, or to share how God has used this book in your life, please write to Elizabeth at:

Jim and Elizabeth George Ministries
P.O. Box 2879
Belfair, WA 98528

Toll-free fax/phone: 1-800-542-4611
www.elizabethgeorge.com
www.jimgeorge.com

∼

Another great book from author Elizabeth George

Scripture–based principles for every reader who wants to become God's woman of excellence.

A Woman After God's Own Heart®

For any woman who wants to achieve a growing relationship with God, develop an active partnership with her husband, and make her home into a spiritual oasis. Study guide included.

A Woman After God's Own Heart®
is available at your local Christian bookstore
or can be ordered from:

Jim and Elizabeth George Ministries
P.O. Box 2879
Belfair, WA 98528
Toll-free fax/phone: 1-800-542-4611
www.elizabethgeorge.com

Books by Elizabeth George

Beautiful in God's Eyes—The Treasures of the Proverbs 31 Woman
Encouraging Words for a Woman After God's Own Heart
God's Wisdom for a Woman's Life
Life Management for Busy Women
Loving God with All Your Mind
Powerful Promises™ for Every Woman
The Remarkable Women of the Bible
A Wife After God's Own Heart
A Woman After God's Own Heart®
A Woman After God's Own Heart® Deluxe Edition
A Woman After God's Own Heart® Audiobook
A Woman After God's Own Heart® Prayer Journal
A Woman's High Calling
A Woman's Walk with God
A Young Woman After God's Own Heart

Growth & Study Guides

God's Wisdom for a Woman's Life Growth & Study Guide
Life Management for Busy Women Growth & Study Guide
Powerful Promises™ for Every Woman Growth & Study Guide
The Remarkable Women of the Bible Growth & Study Guide
A Wife After God's Own Heart Growth & Study Guide
A Woman After God's Own Heart® Growth & Study Guide
A Woman's High Calling Growth & Study Guide
A Woman's Walk with God Growth & Study Guide

A Woman After God's Own Heart® Study Series

BIBLE STUDIES FOR BUSY WOMEN

"God wrote the Bible to change hearts and lives. Every study in this series is written with that in mind—and is specially focused on helping Christian women know how God desires for them to live."
—Elizabeth George

Sharing wisdom gleaned from more than 20 years as a women's Bible study teacher, Elizabeth has prepared insightful lessons that can be completed in 15 to 20 minutes per day. Each lesson includes thought-provoking questions and insights, Bible study tips, instructions for leading a discussion group, and a "heart response" section to make the Bible passage more personal.

Proverbs 31 0-7369-0818-8

Philippians 0-7369-0289-9

1 Peter 0-7369-0290-2

1 Timothy 0-7369-0665-7

Judges/Ruth 0-7369-0498-0

Esther 0-7369-0489-1

James 0-7369-0490-5

Life of Mary 0-7369-0300-3

Life of Sarah 0-7369-0301-1